Circling Hope

JENA BOLES

Inspiring Voices®
A Service of **Guideposts**

Inspiring Voices books may be ordered through booksellers or by contacting:

Inspiring Voices
1663 Liberty Drive
Bloomington, IN 47403
www.inspiringvoices.com
1-(866) 697-5313

ISBN: 978-1-4624-0194-9 (e)
ISBN: 978-1-4624-0195-6 (sc)

Library of Congress Control Number: 2012941889

Printed in the United States of America

Inspiring Voices rev. date: 6/28/2012

Table of Contents

Introduction

How much does your bag weigh? You know, the one you've been stuffing all your junk into for decades. Failure. Loss. Rejection. These are some pretty heavy words, especially when you carry them with you everyday of your life, everywhere you go. Most people can easily identify the cause of their pain, but letting go of it and moving forward are the difficult tasks. Do you honestly realize how your negative experiences (past or present) are hitching a ride on your shoulders and affecting every area of your life? Can you even comprehend how they are holding you back from realizing God's best for you? Take just a moment and ask yourself this question: What would your life look like if you no longer carried your burdens and gave up personal control of your future? I'm not asking you to forget your past, because that is unrealistic. I am asking you, however, to seriously dig through your collection of hurts, view each item for what it really is, and then let the Lord carry your load for you. He desires more than anything, for you to seek Him out and invite Him to direct your steps.

This book is my bag. Within these crisp pages are the very personal contents of my life, strewn publically about for all to examine. I am not proud of much of the subject matter and it nearly crippled me to relive these events in order to get them all down on paper, but there is a purpose for it all. There is a purpose for my transparency and mission to share. Through my darkness comes light. Through my pain comes joy. Through my misery comes HOPE. HOPE for me and HOPE for you. If you are ready to lighten your load and move forward with a new, life-transforming perspective, please walk gently with me through my journey.

One: The Storm of Divorce

Have you ever noticed how many white houses there are in your neighborhood? Perhaps you currently live in a nice little white house with a pretty white fence out front, or maybe your neighbor two houses down and across the street lives in a rickety, old, white house and everyone thinks it's an eyesore. Maybe you're planning to re-side your house in the near future and you're thinking, "White might be nice. You can't go wrong with white." Let's just say there are a whole lot of white houses in this world, and growing up I had the opportunity to live in several of them; one white house after another. I must admit, though, I do have a favorite. If my four-year-old memory logged it right, I'd say it was a big, square farmhouse on a humble acreage about a mile and a half from one of the nicest little midwestern towns you'd ever find. I sure do like to think about that first white house. You see the four short years I lived there were the only years I ever dwelt with a full family unit; father, mother, two brothers, and me. I, the round-faced, little girl with long, dirty blond hair, was the baby of the family; there were four years separating each of us siblings. Being the youngest, my age and innocence shielded me from much of what was happening around me. I was a carefree child, loved by my parents, siblings and everyone around me, as far as my spunky little mind could tell.

Although I don't have an abundance of memories from early childhood (birth to age four), the memories I do have are fond ones. I recall building twine-string forts in our grove with my brothers, gathering fresh vegetables from the garden with my mother, and feeding our "petting zoo" of farm animals with my father. On one feeding occasion, I heartily enjoyed a feast of pig pellets, thinking they were my common breakfast food! Gross, I know, but somehow I survived. I also recall playing in my beloved "outdoor kitchen." From as early as my mind will let me go, I had claimed as my own a giant (by four-year-old standards) old tree on the edge of our grove. The trunk split into a V very low to the ground, low enough for an imaginative kid to steady a well-used frying pan and spatula between. With the loose bark and miscellaneous tree debris, I cooked up some delicious entrees, just like my mommy! These and other precious memories are what make this time of my life the most heartwarming. Life was simple. I woke up. I played. I ate. I got scrubbed clean. I slept. Repeat. LIFE WAS SIMPLE.

The simple life didn't stay simple for long, though. As kindergarten approached, so did the divorce of my parents. I was much too young to understand how this would affect the rest of my life, but I now see it was the very beginning of the brokenness that would invade my heart for years to come. This disruption of God's design for the family unit was the start of all things painful.

Shortly after my first school year had begun, there was one memorable bus ride home that permanently changed my and my siblings' lives. My oldest brother looked out the dusty bus window as we approached our driveway and witnessed his bedroom set going down the road in the back of a pickup truck. Then, once we stepped off the bus, we all realized the gist of the situation. My mother was packing up the house and moving her and us kids into town. I knew very few details of the cause for the divorce. Financial reasons and arguments were definitely part of it, but at such a young age, I was oblivious to what caused the demise of their union. I don't know how much my older brothers were aware of the circumstances leading up to this, but I'm sure they regretfully had to experience a lot more of the unstable atmosphere than I did. However, I do know one fact; the proverbial storm that raged on that sunny afternoon altered and complicated my life and the lives of many forever. My mother and father broke their vows and began new directions in their lives--separately. Sadly, a larger division was drawn in our family as my oldest brother and I ended up moving with our mother, and my other brother decided to move with our father. Parents were divorced. Children were divorced. Unity as I had known it was gone.

Going forward, a new design was established for our family, and my mother was determined to create a stable life as we ventured out on our own. Although I know she was struggling in many ways during this difficult new beginning, she did her very best to balance our days with love, faith, and security. She shuttled us to church every Sunday morning and to weekday church lessons as well. Though we were very poor, she provided a warm, loving home with all the necessary securities of life. She guided our lives as a mother should, but still, there wasn't a blanket big enough to wrap all of the hurt in. There wasn't an embrace warm enough to bring us all together again.

As time and distance came between family members, further divisions were formed. My middle brother, who chose to live with my father, became somewhat of a stranger to me. Though he had doted on me the most since the day I was born, he was now unfamiliar to my days, as he and my father lived hours away. He had been such a friend and buddy of mine up until the end of the divorce, and not having him around anymore caused painful and lingering sadness in my heart. Not every big brother would willingly braid his little sister's hair or spend countless hours playing games and go exploring together as pals. I was not a nuisance to him as younger siblings can sometimes be. He just loved me and loved being with me. He never made me feel like he didn't want me around, but now he was gone from my day-to-day life and I missed him terribly. We all missed him. But he was a soft-hearted young boy who also loved his father and did not want to see him living alone. Therefore, he made a hard choice.

I wish I knew more details surrounding my parents' divorce. I wonder if my mother knew the decision to end her marriage would also mean somewhat of an end to her relationship with her middle child. No matter from which angle you look at it, hearts were broken all the way around.

As I continued to grow, my mother's evident dislike for my father stained my own heart as well. I felt as though I was inadvertently being taught to dislike someone I barely knew (which planted in me seeds of disrespect and inadequacy toward men in general). I grew up seeing very little of my father and my beloved brother--just a holiday now and then. We had pleasant visits when they took place, but life was so very disconnected. My strong and courageous mother was trying to fill the roles of both mother and father for two children, and my strong and courageous father was trying to fill the roles of mother and father to yet another child. Unfortunately, my disassembled family would set the example for all my future relationships.

Two: Taking Her Home

When I was around six years of age, my mother summoned my oldest brother and me to the kitchen table, but not for a tantalizing meal. Instead, we were served a healthy dose of reality that poisoned our lives forever—*cancer*. My mother revealed she had been diagnosed with breast cancer. I later found out she had had lumps for several years before she actually got them checked, and now the reality of it all was coming full circle. She explained how she would undergo all sorts of chemotherapy treatments, experimental treatments, lifestyle/healthy eating changes, and so on, and she honestly believed she would be cured. She was a fighter. She was a single mother with two children under her roof. To die was not an option. As she faced this new reality, she opened up her Bible, folded her hands, and dug deep into God's Word for comfort and direction.

As months and years passed by, a mastectomy, hip replacement (as the cancer spread) and many other procedures were performed. Each surgery and recovery period rolled into the next and over the years we all grew very weary from the rollercoaster of highs and lows. Unfortunately, never did the words "I'm cured" show up. I can't imagine what life must have been like for my mother during this time. I can't imagine the fear of leaving her children behind as she endured surgery after surgery and hospital stay after hospital stay. I also can't imagine what life must have been like for my two brothers and my father during this time, which is why I can only share my own experiences.

In elementary school, I always felt like the "different kid" for whom people felt sorry. I was not the prettiest child, didn't have the nicest clothes or newest toys and certainly didn't come from a normal home of the 1980s. I came from a broken home with a dying mother. However, like small communities and churches always do, they wrapped their loving arms around our family and helped out in countless ways. Meals were continually delivered, special gifts around the holidays always seemed to arrive and numerous people were always available to help. The most difficult issue for me was being shifted in and out of other people's homes whenever my mother was too sick to care for me. I generally spent about two weeks with each family before switching to another temporary home. All the while, I prayed I could simply go back to my own familiar surroundings with the mother I adored. Don't get me wrong, some of the most wonderful families took me in and treated me as if I were their own, but there still was no real sense of ~HOME~. I always felt like extra baggage in the family's normal lives. I missed MY family. I missed MY mother who I had grown even closer to as she solely nurtured my delicate, young mind. Somehow, however, even through the feelings of longing and uncertainty there were still several happy experiences during this era (age 5-10) and for that I am grateful. Regardless, the positive experiences were never quite enough to stop me from feeling…a little lost in it all.

Then after several years of fighting the ferocious cancer, my mother's battle finally came to an end. The Lord decided it was time for my precious mother to go home; to be free from pain, free from struggles; to just be free. With only 37 years in her book of life on earth, three children and a host of other friends and family said goodbye to this amazing woman. Again, I cannot speak for my siblings or for anyone else. I cannot tell you what this felt like in the hearts of all those who loved her. I can only tell you how it felt to me, as a ten year old, floundering young girl. I can only tell you how it changed me, how it severed my heart, how it handicapped my tender, young life and left me broken.

After my mother's death, I initially went to live with a friend of my mother's. This friend had a large family, offered a loving, Christian home and did so much for me during the short time I lived there. This new living arrangement, however, meant switching schools. I was not at all excited about this, but I had no other choice. I needed a stable home with stable parents. Then halfway through my fifth grade school year, my father came back into my life and desired for me to live with him and my brother… permanently. I did not desire to move in with my father at all. I felt like I barely knew him and the picture of him painted in my brain by my mother was very fresh. Though my firm resentment for him may have been unfair, it was real and lasting.

Again, I don't truly know what went on between my mother and father that caused all of their turmoil. I only knew at this point, I was scared to live with my father. I didn't fear him in a physical sense, but he was much like a stranger to me. How could this stranger of a father possibly compare to the warm and loving mother I freshly grieved for so deeply? I was once again lost and floating aimlessly through my days. I was confused, angry and crushed by it all. Why? The question was always why? I found myself daydreaming on many occasions about what life might be like in a "normal" home with both my parents and all three of us siblings together. I felt as though nothing in my life had been normal thus far and everything about my current situation was uncertain. The direction of my life seemed to change like the wind, and I was simply along for the ride.

The final decision making factor in going to live with my father and my brother, was simply....my brother. The brother who had doted on me as a very young child and who had also become a stranger to me, still held such a dear place in my heart. That deep connection with him that I missed so much finally swayed my heart and brought me to my next living arrangement. On to the next home I moved and on to the next school I went. Unfortunately, the older I got the harder it was to change schools. Friendship circles among fellow students had long since been established and I never really seemed to fit in to one particular crowd. I was placed among a body of people who didn't know my past and didn't understand my immediate grief. Aside from the school issues, I had no idea what to expect from my father's parental role. He was a hard worker, really rough around the edges, and found it very difficult to show tenderness or communicate love to a pre-teen girl. Thankfully, my brother did. He was a GIFT in my life! He was my brother, my father, my mother, my friend and my counselor all rolled into one. Looking back, I am still just amazed by the human being he chose to be....to ME. He too was grieving the loss of his mother and living a very difficult life in a broken home, but he was the kind of person who was born with the disposition to overcome. He was just one of those easy-going people who possessed an innate gift to make the most of everything. Unfortunately, I possessed a different disposition.

Three: Coping Mechanisms

Like many teenage girls, I was struggling with my physical image and personal worth. I did not live in an environment where self-esteem was promoted, nor did I feel as though I had any structure or guidance from the person who was supposed to be parenting me. Regardless of my brother's efforts to "raise" me, it was a role too big for him as he was just a teenager himself. Day after day I felt unsupported and misunderstood within what should have been my haven, my ~HOME~. In my father's defense, he simply didn't know how to provide that environment and he was doing the best he could as a single father. I, however, was processing a lot of hurt and confusion from the first decade of my life and didn't know what to do with all my questions and emotions.

I did try to involve myself in school activities/sports etc. but those areas of my overly-dysfunctional life also made me feel like a failure. Consequently, I took all of the messy, hurtful feelings I was dealing with and at the age of twelve years I started my bulimia "career". A few years earlier, I had heard about an older girl doing this and for some reason it now seemed like a twisted and legitimate way to control my physical image and serve as somewhat of an outlet for my internal pain. Quite frankly, I just felt like a lost mess, because that's what I was. I put on a good show of normalcy for a few interested teachers and adults/friends close to me, but inside I was screaming for....love, affection, guidance, structure, and worth.

From there, I started other self-destructive habits. I earned my first minor for consuming alcohol at age twelve and also started seeking the attention of the opposite sex in age-inappropriate ways. I was grasping for ways to fit in and be liked/loved! As a result, alcohol and partying became the main focus of my teen years and surprisingly, the adults around me didn't seem to think it was that big of a deal...so neither did I.

With high school came yet another transition. My father remarried and relocated us to yet another new town, new school, new friends etc. The twist on this relocation was that my brother (my biggest supporter in life) did not move with us. He still had one year of high school left and, understandably, did not want to move away. My father, however, was solely focused on his own new life ahead of him, and agreed to leave my brother behind. As a result, my brother therefore spent his last year of high school living with friends in the area. My father had basically thrown him into adulthood in every sense of the word which is also similar to what had happened to my oldest brother after my mother's death. He too had been left to live with friends near his high school in order to complete his senior year. Unity was simply a foreign word in our family. Though two adults had chosen to marry and have children, it seemed either no one was left or either no one was interested in finishing raising us. Kids and adults always seemed to be going in different directions.

Then to add to the chaos of living arrangements, my father's new wife had a daughter who was in my same grade which required the blending of families as well. From then on, it felt as though I was constantly being compared; within our home, school, sports etc. By this time, basically everyone knew about my relationship with bulimia as well as my drinking habits and yet no one forcibly stepped in. No one in an adult role said enough is enough and earnestly tried to change what was going on. I knew what I was doing was inappropriate and unhealthy, but I couldn't stop. My world was full of chaos and confusion, yet my habits were my coping mechanisms to somehow deal with it all. Needless to say, there was a battle raging between my father and me, my new step-family and me and within myself as well, and I was just simply not coping with any of it.

Again, my show of semi-normalcy on the outside hid a lot of things from a lot of people. The lies I told about the scars on my wrists kept others from knowing just how bad I was hurting and how far I was willing to go in order to end life as I knew it. The lies I told about the hundreds of missing pills from our medicine cabinet also kept others from realizing still more attempts to end my life. I was completely sick of living my chaotic life and was not interested in seeing what the future had in store. I was tired of being bulimic, unloved, uncared for, ridiculed and feeling hopeless.

The one act to finally stir a shift of events was my father's choice to divorce his new wife. Again, here was displayed another example of a broken relationship, but this did bring the household count down to two; my father and I. Because of this, we formed somewhat of an alliance with each other. I felt like he was a little more interested in me and I could sense his need to be comforted as well. But just like everything in my life, nothing stayed the same for very long. It didn't take more than a few months until he reached out and began another relationship. This time, it was with an old flame of his living about two hours away. She was a good person and I was happy for him, but now my father was gone to his new girlfriend's house from Friday night until Sunday night nearly every single weekend. I had zero guidance or supervision. Needless to say, "family time" was not something that ever existed in my life. Just as my brothers had felt deserted during their last years of high school, I too felt similar emotions. This freedom seemed alright to me as a 16 year old, but it also got me into a lot of trouble and unsafe environments. The lack of parental interest in my life coupled with my extremely low self-esteem and broken moral compass led me straight into a path of unhealthy relationships and unacceptable choices. My mother was gone, my brother was off on his own now, my father was solely focused on the newest direction of his life, and I was back to square one feeling lost and abandoned.

Four: New Beginnings/
Final Endings

Next up, High School Graduation! I had no idea what I wanted to do with my life, but I had somehow managed to get pretty descent grades in high school and I knew I wanted to pursue a college degree. My father had not pursued a college education and there were certainly no expectations from him with regard to what I would do with my life. As my sole, living parent, he offered no direction, guidance and certainly no financial support for college. Just as they had been for several years, all choices were left up to me. Nevertheless, I registered to attend a state university and I felt like maybe this was going to be the fresh start I so desperately needed. My father's new girlfriend made sure I received a very nice high school graduation open house and I felt as though I was somewhat capable of moving forward with my own (adult) life in a positive direction.

Needless to say, that path of positive direction lasted a whole two weeks. Just two weeks after graduation, my father was once again gone to his girlfriend's house for the weekend. While he was absent, I hosted a small, drunken gathering with a few classmates. After everyone had left, I (so typically) passed out on our living room couch. As the festivities had gone late into the night, I was in no shape to answer the echoing knock on the front door at 7:00am the next morning. I tried to ignore the sound, but whoever was knocking was persistent and continued on. Finally, I opened the door ever so slowly and was greeted by a very somber policeman and a pastor. Initially, I thought I was in some sort of trouble and was preparing myself for a fine, lecture or some sort of punishment stemming from my underage, drunken behavior. To my surprise, this was not the case at all as they proceeded to ask if they could come in and visit with me about a very saddening event that had taken place during the night. Although I was scared and unsure, I allowed them to come in. Upon entering, they were greeted by ashtrays and beer cans everywhere. The house reeked of alcohol and smoke as did I. As the fullness of my hangover was quickly settling in, I welcomed their suggestion that I sit down.

At seventeen years old, I did not know what the presence of a policeman and a pastor signified. I quickly learned, however, and would never forget the news they delivered for the rest of my life. My now twenty-one year old brother, who I had been so very close to since the death of my mother--was gone. Actually, the precise word they used was "taken". He was "taken" in an automobile accident during the night. TAKEN! I couldn't even wrap my brain around this concept. How could yet another piece of my family be gone? Shock and disbelief rushed over me as I tried to process the unspeakable news.

After finally gaining a tiny bit of composure, they proceeded to ask for my father's location and I managed to give them his girlfriend's address. Now on the search to locate and inform my father, the policeman left and the pastor asked if he could stay and pray with me for awhile. Honestly, it really didn't matter to me either way as nothing other than heartache was even registering in my brain. I was shaking and crying uncontrollably. As I had no idea who this pastor was, his words were falling on deaf ears. Basically every ounce of faith I had once possessed had taken a backseat in my life after the death of my mother, and being as biblically unreceptive as I was, this man may as well have been speaking Chinese. It just simply felt as if my heart was going to explode at any moment. After a few minutes, the pastor did in fact leave as well and I was left alone to process this newest catastrophic event in my young life. Being alone and feeling abandoned was nothing new for me, but now I was alone, in shock, still intoxicated and utterly heartbroken. I rolled on the living room floor sobbing in angst for what seemed like hours. Every hurtful emotion from my seventeen years of loss, abandonment, shame, ridicule and worthlessness came to a culmination in my heart. Why? Again the question, why is this all happening to me? My life-cycle of grief, heartache and hopelessness seemed as though it would never end. Like never before, my spirit felt essentially crushed.

As time continued to march on, the funeral inevitably came and went in a blur. Of course hundreds of grief stricken family and friends were reeling from the news but I was only capable of thinking of myself; drowning in my own sorrows. I had selfishly always looked only at the negatives in MY life, processed them in unhealthy ways, and blamed everyone else for my fate. I certainly wasn't the only person in the world who had divorced parents or who had lost multiple family members, but as my selfish nature reared its ugly head I only seemed to care about myself and my own feelings.

This newest devastating event only catapulted my bulimia, binge drinking and depression into high gear. As I forced myself to glance at the future, I knew I had the summer to process these emotions before college would start and I began by moving out of my father's home and into my grandmother's lake cabin several hours away. The transition of moving out went quite smoothly. I was basically used to living on my own already as I had purchased and prepared all of my own food, did all my own laundry, financially supported myself (by holding down two jobs) and came and went as I pleased while living with my father. Essentially, we had been part-time roommates during my last two years of high school. Now that I had ventured out fully on my own, I was looking to ESCAPE life as I had known it thus far. I was on a mission to live in a fantasy world as if everything were ok. I really didn't even process the huge loss that had just taken place, but rather chose to pretend it never happened.

After the move, I kept busy with my new job at a local pizza place and I developed a few friendships with locals my age. I tried to forget everything that had happened in my life and I focused now more than ever on controlling my weight (as I religiously walked several miles every day) and drank my cares away every opportunity I had. I managed to have a lot of so-called fun that summer amidst the pain of grieving, because I chose not to live in reality. I spent time with some amazing people who were very accepting of me and gave me a taste of what it felt like to be a normal care-free teenager. There was no ridicule or judgment from them. They were just good people and to this day they hold very special places in my heart. Without them, I'm not sure I would have made it through those first delusional months of despair. The summer, however, did inevitably come to an end and life moved forward.

With the help of a loving aunt and my dad's girlfriend, I did proceed to move into the college dorms that fall. I still had no idea what I would choose for a career, but I figured I had a couple years to get my generals done before I had to seriously figure it out. Financially, I had no income after the summer job had ceased, but since I had just turned eighteen, I had received my mother's life insurance benefits. Her choice to give me this financial gift would make it possible to pay for at least two years of college. Just coming off the somewhat positive summer I had experienced, I was feeling a little stronger as classes began and yet another school/living transition took place. For the most part, I started off on the right track, devoting the majority of my focus to studying and trying to establish new friendships. I wanted desperately to fit in and simply be liked. Friendships/ relationships, however, had always been difficult for me. I was very secretive about my personal habits because everything always revolved around being able to throw up whenever I felt I "needed" to. If I couldn't control anything else in my life, I felt that at least I could control my weight. I therefore chose to tell a lot of lies and play a lot of mind games in order to be perceived as "normal". Regardless of the difficulties my relationships caused, I still always seemed to latch onto some guy some where as life revolved around wanting/needing someone to love me and pay attention to me.

Unsurprisingly, it only took a couple of months before I did just that and decided to move off campus. Not only did I move off campus to follow my latest dysfunctional relationship, but I also moved out of town about twenty miles away. The distance from college life did not help my focus at all and only enabled me to live the drunken life-style I was all too familiar with. As I did in high school, I managed to get fairly decent grades my first year of college, but my on and off again relationship combined with my drinking habits soon drastically changed the events of my life.

At nineteen years old, I received my first D.W.I (driving while intoxicated). I had been drinking in a bar in a neighboring town (underage of course) and had attempted to drive myself home that night. I didn't make it far however, until I went off the road, hit a large rock and finally came to a stop at the bottom of a very steep embankment. It was pouring rain that night and the ditch had quite a bit of water in it. I tried calling the on again off again boyfriend with my cell phone, but I was so drunk I had no idea where I was. I didn't know what road I was on and couldn't give out any directions. While I eventually just passed out in my stranded vehicle, he and his father spent several hours during the night looking for me. Unfortunately, their efforts were in vain and it was a nearby farmer who knocked on my window the next morning and woke me up. He had noticed the tracks going off the road and stopped to check the area. It didn't take him long to assess what had happened as I reeked of alcohol and had plenty left in the vehicle as well. The kind man then offered me a ride home and I gratefully and still-drunkenly accepted. However, another passerby had contacted the sheriff's office in the meantime fearing someone needed medical help. To my dismay, an officer arrived on the scene before we were able to leave, and there was no escaping the deserved outcome. I could have easily killed myself, or more importantly, someone else. The problem was I didn't see it that way at the time.

You see I only associated with people who drank and condoned my behavior. Therefore, the expensive fine, loss of license and one-day alcohol class didn't slow my extra-curricular life down one bit. It did, however, bring my fleeting college career to a screeching halt. I was about three fourths of the way through my second year of college, but because of my latest award I no longer had a way to transport myself to and from class. A few teachers were willing to work with me and allowed me to complete my courses before my full driving permits were revoked, but I simply had to drop out of all my other classes.

I of course felt like a huge failure, but that feeling was nothing new.

With the new turn of events, my college career was traded in for a full-time position at a medical clinic in the small town I lived in. I was able to walk to and from work and earn just enough money to cover my living expenses (rent, utilities, food to throw up and alcohol to consume). My co-workers soon discovered my destructive habits and voiced their sincere concerns, but there wasn't much they could do for me. There wasn't much anyone could do for me. I was on a downward spiral, and not even I realized just how far down I had gone. I was at my complete breaking point.

Five: Enough

Then on a Sunday evening while surprisingly completely sober, I sat quietly in my apartment mulling over the mess I had made of my life. Being sober that night meant facing reality without the delusions of an altered state of mind. As I hauntingly stumbled through my thoughts, I relived the alcohol offence that had completely changed the course of my adult life. I focused on the holes left in my heart from the death of my mother and my brother. I pondered how life might have been different if they were both still alive, and I felt like, if only my mother would've been able to raise me under her ideals of love and structure than maybe I wouldn't have ended up this way? Regardless, it was much too late for the "what ifs". The past was over, the damage was done, and I saw nothing in my future worth living for. I was sick of the pathetic life encompassing me and I wanted out.

After hours of irrationally battling the past and present in my mind, I made a choice. I made a choice to change everything. I made a final choice to die. I didn't write any goodbyes or attempt to warn anyone, I just methodically started the series of events that would hopefully end my life. I got in my vehicle and drove (without a license or insurance) approximately 20 miles to the scene of my brother's life-ending accident. It was an area of rolling pastures and deadly drop offs should one veer off the road. Silence filled the car and I remember telling myself over and over in my mind, "Don't turn back. Don't go back to your life. You hate everything about your pathetic life. You hate yourself. You are a worthless human being. Just keep on driving." I therefore pressed on and increased my speed as I raced closer and closer to the "Think/Accident" sign that marked the area where my brother had been "taken" just two years earlier. I then proceeded to launch my car off the same drop-off that had instantly killed my brother; in the hopes it would have the same effect on me. As the car landed explosively, I clenched the steering wheel so hard it broke. I slammed my head into the windshield and cracked it as well. I had immediate pain in my lower back, and because I could feel all these sensations, I was extremely angry. I...was not dead! I WAS NOT DEAD!?!? I could now add this most bold and horrific suicide attempt to my list of failures. Why? I asked again. Why can't it all just come to an end? Nothing in my existence made me want to be alive, yet something/someone had kept me here.

After the minor injuries healed and the smoke cleared from all the gossip, I settled right back into my pathetic life. Honestly, I had walked this path for so long now that I didn't know any other way to live. Misery and self-destruction seemed to follow me wherever I went, whatever I did. With all my issues, I became a hopeless burden to the few friends and family close to me, and I decided it was time to once again move away (run away) from my dead-end life. I thought if I at least moved away from the small town that knew so much, I could put some of the past behind me and open a new door to the future.

After months and months of saving, I had enough money to get my license back and insure my vehicle. Now that I was independently mobile, I was able to take that next step in "running away" as I then moved to a little bit bigger town and found another apartment, job etc. Even as I began to meet a few new and kind people, I still felt the urgency to play the same old secrecy games. There were just too many things about my life that others didn't want or need to know, and I wasn't about to advertise my shame. Time and time again I asked myself, "What would people think of me if they truly knew just how messed up I really was?" Yet somehow even through my deceptiveness, those new friendships were what saved me and kept me hanging on by a thread. Ultimately, however, my self-destructive habits of drinking and binging/purging did not change in my new surroundings and still controlled every area of my life.

Consequently, at the age of twenty-one years I proceeded to earn my second D.W.I. award. From this additional costly offence, I lost my license for a year, spent a weekend in jail, thirty days on house arrest, and several months under court supervision. I also had to pay a huge fine and was once again the subject of public ridicule. Shame oozed from every pore of my body as I furthered my qualifications as the poster child for failure. With every move I made, I was sinking in dishonesty and denial. I was not truthful with anyone about my life; I did not value or honor relationships; I had no regard for authority or laws, and I focused solely on myself and the downward spiral I was traveling. Nothing in my newest venture had positively changed the trajectory of my life.

Still through all the new turmoil, I found myself seeking out even more of my typical rescue-relationships (yes, I mean plural relationships and sometimes at the same time). My twisted view of relationships basically consisted of searching for another individual to rescue me from my life and make me happy. If I wasn't happy, I'd simply move on to another candidate who appeared to offer me something better or something more. I desperately wanted someone, anyone, to bring joy to my life and worth to my existence.

Sadly, my warped longing left me constantly searching for someone to change me; someone to make me not hate myself. As a result of this longing, my next relationship seemed to fit the bill to a tee. It was pretty much like every other I'd ever had, except this time it involved direct ties to my "taken" brother who I missed terribly. This time, I reconnected with an old friend of his and I clung (and I mean CLUNG) to the idea it would be different. I obviously possessed a deep desire to change and be a completely different type of a person, and I found myself pondering the "desperate times call for desperate measures" theory. Therefore when the "issue" of marriage came up, it seemed like the next appropriate (desperate) measure.

Maybe marriage was what it would take for me to grow up and change my ways. I was now 24 years old. I was certainly old enough to marry and was more than ready to move (run) in a different direction. Although I desperately wanted my life to date and unhealthy habits to disappear, it just…wasn't that easy. Nothing had ever been easy and I don't know why I thought this time would be different. The first issue within this wannabe-new-and-improved relationship (and subsequent marriage) was that it still revolved completely around drinking and partying. I, of course, had connected myself to someone with many of my similar habits and that was and had always been a recipe for disaster. The only habit that truly did change through this union was my twelve year (age 12-24) battle with bulimia. My new husband was grossly mortified by it, as he should have been, and basically demanded I stop. In the past, no one close to me had ever reacted this way to my disgusting coping mechanism and over time, I did finally quit. After stopping, it took nearly two more years for the bulimia induced swelling in my face to go down. My face literally took on a whole new shape and people who hadn't seen me in quite awhile were taken aback. Miraculously, I had taken a step in a positive direction.

Regardless of my grand achievement, many other issues still surrounded my marriage; financial instability, irresponsible behavior and of course ALCOHOL. Then to add to the chaos, (drum roll please) I got pregnant. Honestly, this news to me was devastating.

Growing up, I initially had no desire to ever get married and certainly never to have children. Over time, I had convinced myself I was somewhat worthy of being a wife (even though I was terrible at it), but I had not convinced myself I was worthy of being a mother. I was VERY selfish and quite frankly, I was scared to death. What if this child was like me? I could barely stand myself and I didn't want to pass my own miserable life onto a beautiful, innocent child. I felt as though I had nothing good to offer this new life growing inside of me, and the fear of the unknown consumed my thoughts.

This same fear, however, sank deep enough into my heart for me to get serious about my physical pregnancy health. Thankfully, I did stop drinking as soon as I knew I was pregnant and I tried my best to eat as healthy as I knew how. Still, it took me at least half the pregnancy to find any joy in the experience at all. At around week twenty in the pregnancy, it was revealed a precious baby girl was taking shape within me. The incredible ultrasound images brought reality to it all and little by little I began to accept the fact I was going to be a mother. I-was-going-to-be-a-MOTHER! I was still so scared though that my child's life would be like my own and those fears truly haunted me.

When this most precious and perfect child finally emerged from my body, I was in awe of her. I was amazed at her purity and innocence and I was overcome with love and fear all at the same time. Like many new mothers, I wasn't overly confident in knowing just how to handle everything. I did have a handful of people who supported me and who I felt comfortable asking questions, but I second guessed myself constantly. I also felt my husband second-guessed my skills as well, and that made me feel even more inadequate. Needless to say, my feelings of inadequacy and failure were deeply engraved in my being and I just couldn't move beyond them. As the days turned into weeks and the weeks to months, my lack of motherly confidence steered me back to my old habits. My selfish desires for the pre-pregnancy freedom I had known drove me back to alcohol and back to irresponsible living. As I began drinking again, I focused more and more on me and less and less on my family. Not surprisingly, the unhealthy habits that had brought my husband and me together also tore us apart in many ways. The drinking and partying weakened the structure of our commitment and left the door wide open for failure. Also, my husband's choice to pursue a work opportunity that took him away from home (except on weekends) brought any sense of unity to an end. I was lonely and once again…ready to run.

As stated in earlier chapters of this book, I had not witnessed long-committed marriages growing up and honestly, I never approached my own marriage as being something that would never end. Relationships were completely conditional to me. Actually, my whole life was conditional. If something didn't work, than I'd run from it and try to find a new or more self-fulfilling situation. I'd find another relationship or town to move to etc. If I thought a better life was somewhere else down the road than I'd start walking (or running), and it was time for me to get moving. After nearly four and a half years of wedded dysfunction, I was done. My husband did make some attempts at the end to create change, but my mind was made up.

I absolutely, one hundred percent wanted out. I packed up my two year old daughter and I and we moved into a one bedroom apartment in a nearby town. The place was so small we were literally living on top of each other, but at least I felt free and in control. That was all that really mattered to me. Within just a few months of living on my own again, I managed to scrounge up some money to pay for the divorce and never second guessed the decision.

Nothing in my life had worked out the way I had hoped or dreamed, and I consequently became a 29 year old single mother who had failed at basically everything I had ever done in life, including marriage and motherhood. Parts of my past struggles and heartaches were not caused by me, but by death and grief, yet many others were solely my fault. They were simply the outcome of my choices; the outcome of my attitude. My selfishness, grief, insecurity and shame had dictated every path I had taken and brought me to this next fork in the road.

INNER-MISSION:

At this time, I want to take a little break from my journey to give you a chance to reflect on all the struggles I've shared and how parts of my story might currently mirror your own life. Can you see yourself anywhere in the storyline unfolding? Maybe there are only similarities in our lives and your story involves a few other twists and turns, but have you ever experienced any of these same feelings or situations? Perhaps it's a daughter, brother, mother or a good friend you see in this same pattern of unhealthy, broken and unstable living. Whether it's you or someone you love, I want you to understand this: Life-can-change! There is a way to end the vicious cycle of despair and heartache and it starts by ingesting a life-altering dose of HOPE. You/They desperately need HOPE and HOPE is what the second half of this book is all about. Make no mistake; the blessing of HOPE comes from our great God and He wishes for you to bask in the glory won on the cross by the death and resurrection of His son, Jesus Christ. No matter what you have done or experienced in your life to date, you are worthy of receiving God's best for your future. You are worthy! You have meaning and purpose and because the Lord fully instructed me to "tell my story", I know He intends to use the very personal experiences detailed in this book to give HOPE and new life to those in need.

As you gather your thoughts and personal recollections of your journey, I ask that you would do a little exercise for me. If there are any words or concepts listed below that are engraved in your being and are holding you back every day of your life, would you take a pen or pencil and put a line through them? Please don't circle them, just put a line through them and recognize the stronghold they have on you. I want you to sincerely dig through your past and your present and acknowledge each word affecting you in one way or another. If you don't see the precise burdening word(s) representing the condition of your heart either now or in the past, please add it to the list and put a line through it as well.

Selfishness	Shame	Loss
Insecurity	Grief	Alcoholism
Addiction	Rejection	Depression
Suicide	Ridicule	Despair
Eating Disorder	Unlovable	Unwanted
Abandonment	Divorce	Failure
Humiliation	Forgotten	Broken
Imperfect	Unfaithful	Dishonesty

_____

_____

_____

_____

_____

_____

_____

_____

_____

_____

I know this process is difficult and it causes you to relive the most hurtful parts of your existence, and I understand the agony this self-examination process creates in your heart. While writing the first half of this book and sharing my pain, I wanted to quit over and over and over again. I constantly asked myself, what will people think of me if they know the whole story of my past? What will my children and my family think of me when they realize how disgusting my life has been? How could the Lord even ask me to tell the world my most shameful experiences and publically reveal the utter brokenness of my heart? And then the answer was given:

~Because the first half of this book is not the end of my story.
~My sin, shame and brokenness no longer define me, but now motivate me.
~My life has been transformed into a beautiful tapestry of love and purpose.
~My heart has been healed and I want that same healing to overflow into you.

"Praise be to the God and Father of our Lord Jesus Christ, the Father of compassion and the God of all comfort, who comforts us in all our troubles, so that we can comfort those in any trouble with the comfort we ourselves receive from God. For just as the sufferings of Christ flow over into our lives, so also through Christ our comfort overflows."
2 Corinthians 1:3-5 NIV

It is by no mistake or coincidence this book has found it's way into your hands. I do not believe in chance. I do, however, believe in the Word of God and the intricate and beautiful life He created for you before you were even born. I believe in the ultimate forgiveness and saving grace freely offered to every individual who repents of their sins and believes in the one, true Jesus Christ as their Lord and Savior, who died on the cross for our sins, ascended into heaven and sits at the right hand of God the Father almighty. I believe in God's purpose and plan for my life, and I believe in His purpose and plan for your life as well. This…is not the end of your story either.

Every hurtful or destructive word you crossed out during the process of self-examination is a feeling or situation God wants lifted from your shoulders. There is no amount of pain or agony that cannot be healed by our great God. He wants to give you a new life in Christ. He wants to mend your brokenness and finally give you peace. Though peace does not mean you will live without affliction or struggle, it does mean you will be given the strength to endure all trials, the courage to live a life solely for Christ, and the promise that you will never walk alone or independently carry your burdens.

"I will give you a new heart and put a new spirit in you; I will remove from you your heart of stone and give you a heart of flesh. And I will put my Spirit in you and move you to follow my decrees and be careful to keep my laws. Then you will live in the land I gave your ancestors; you will be my people, and I will be your God. I will save you from all your uncleanness."
Ezekiel 36:26-38 NIV

Before I get back into my journey and subsequent life-transformation, I want to offer a gentle reminder about sin; my sin, your sin and everyone's sin. No one sin is bigger than another in God's eyes, and His mercy is greater than your greatest sin. There is nothing in your life or another's life that cannot be forgiven, restored and made anew. My life is a testimony to transformation, and I invite you to walk with me through the second half of this book letting the fullness of God's love take up residence in the deepest, most painful crevices of your soul igniting your own process of healing and transformation. There is HOPE!

Six: The Dream

Although I had been baptized as a baby, raised by a Christian mother for the first ten years of my life, confirmed as a teenager and again as an adult in order to join my ex-husband's church, never before had I fallen on my knees before the Lord in the way I was about to fall.

I had spent those first few months on my own with my daughter practicing all the same dysfunctional habits of my past. I knew deep down I had a sincere desire to change, but that desire was always drowned out by guilt and shame. Every day that passed by was another day my daughter was learning from my example and inevitably developing my traits and my way of living. The picture of what her life might become, because of me, was haunting. Also, the realization of how my own life might someday end...haunted me. I was a sinful, selfish and immoral human being and surely my consequence for it all would be the fires of Hell. With all my corrupt life choices weighing heavily on my shoulders, I literally began obsessing over Heaven and Hell and fearing the outcome of my life/death.

As I lay down to sleep one hopeless night, I experienced a dream, a vision that would change my life forever. The setting of the dream was a building similar to a hospital. Like all hospitals, there were many rooms but all the rooms here had large glass windows on every wall. I could see the hundreds and hundreds of people waiting their turn before making their way to the great room. Once our holding room had been ushered along, we were individually placed on stretchers and strapped down. Male and female "nurses" then began issuing each person a series of IVs. With each chemical infused into our bodies, our internal functions began to shut down. Everyone in the building was being put to death slowly and consciously. I was amazed at how calm and accepting all the other people were acting, because that was not my reaction.

I was petrified and literally freaking out. I began wailing and shouting even through the physical and chemical restrictions being placed on my abilities. I screamed "No! No! No! This cannot happen yet! I don't know my fate! I don't know if I'll be sent to Hell or somehow make it into Heaven." I begged, "Please stop! Oh, please stop! I do not want to go to Hell!" And in the blink of an eye, my heavenly mother was there sitting by my stretcher holding my hand and patting my arm gently. With a smile on her face and in the most comforting and calm manner, she said to me, "Honey, you already know. You already know (where you're going)." And then I woke up. I was sobbing as I sat straight up in bed, and I felt as if I'd just run the most physical and mental race of my life. The tears resulting from this abrupt awakening, however, were not the only emotions I was feeling. I was overwhelmed with a sense of peace and HOPE I had never experienced before. I, the poor, miserable sinner knew without a doubt I would be going to HEAVEN one day! Hallelujah! Hallelujah!

God had seen the pain, fear and despair in my heart and used my mother through a dream to change the course of my life forever. I immediately felt a sense of worth and value, which were feelings I had lacked for decades. In the weeks that followed, I found myself focusing on my Baptism and on the Christian roots of my early upbringing that I had long since forgotten. Though I did not know how the rest of my earthly life would unfold, I knew I had a purpose. Never again, would I question my existence or eternal fate. Never... again.

Seven: Priceless Gifts

My day to day life in general did not change in the same blink of an eye (like my dream), but over time I made progress. For the first time in my life, I was improving and moving forward instead of spiraling downward. As I began praying sincerely and faithfully, I was moved to attend church regularly, and I didn't just attend out of a sense of duty; I fully desired to be there! I listened. I clung to every word. I let the power of the Holy Spirit nourish and restore me. I knew, without a doubt, I was heading in a new direction.

In a small, conservative town where divorce is (thankfully) not easily accepted, I quietly walked into church and claimed a space in a pew. I thought I could feel the mental questions and stares from fellow attendees burning right through me, but I knew I was worthy of being there. Even if the congregation didn't feel I belonged there, I knew God wanted me there and that was all that mattered. To my surprise, the congregation welcomed me with open arms. The Pastor welcomed me with open arms. I knew the small-town residents positioned all around me knew full well the status of my life (newly-divorced, sinful, shameful), yet within those sacred walls I did not feel judged. I felt loved and comforted. I felt like part of the family. Finally, I was exactly where I needed to be in order to truly change my ways; safe in the Lord's care. Nothing had ever fulfilled me the way God's love was fulfilling me now. As I stared at the huge cross hanging bolding before me, I began to genuinely trust in the promise of God's word. For the first time in my life, I truly believed Jesus Christ died for ME. Not just for someone else with a much prettier life and upbringing than mine, but for ME and MY sins.

The safety and comfort I experienced from my faith began to create countless changes in my behavior. Over time, I began drinking less and less until I simply didn't even desire "carefree-drunkenness" anymore. I began to see my drunken behaviors for what they really were; temporary escapes from the pain of reality. Drunkenness and partying had also been my selfish attempts to stay free and irresponsible, regardless of my responsibilities as a wife and mother. For once I was facing my pain, grief and ugly habits and I was not placing blame on anyone else. I faced it all head on, and I was certain I was not facing it alone. My great God was with me every step of the way. When I would stumble, He would pick me up and find a way to gently (and sometimes not so gently) get me back on track. I learned to recognize His corrective actions and welcome those instead of fight them, for they only made me grow stronger. Through reading Scripture, I established new standards for myself and my relationships, and I began focusing on strong women of the bible to be my examples. I no longer allowed others to walk all over me or make me feel inadequate, and I stopped constantly seeking the attention/admiration of others in order to feel loved. I had a God who loved me and for the first time in my life, that was enough. The opinions and approval/disapproval of others no longer mattered because I knew…who I was in Christ. I became a Christian first, a mother second and everything else took a number down the line.

With my new standards and personal strength in place, I now possessed a very different outlook on men and relationships. Because I had finally set my Christian relationship standards in stone, I was no longer interested in being romantically involved with anyone who didn't feel the same. I knew that a relationship with a mutual commitment to faith would make all the difference in its strength and longevity. With my unwillingness to compromise my faith, God then gifted me with a man who would ultimately become my husband, my best friend, my partner in life. Not only was he willing to accept my past and see beyond my flaws, but he was willing to walk side by side with me (and the Lord) through whatever the future might bring. Amazingly, this man was not only interested in my life, but equally in my precious daughter's life as well and his patience and kindness overflowed to us both abundantly. God had led me to an incredible, integrity-filled man and I was deeply blessed.

As I continued to honestly and faithfully seek the will of God in my life, it seemed He was now hard at work in every area as doors were opening left and right. Once I invited Him in and finally gave Him total control, He began to change everything! He changed my confidence, my attitude, and my gratitude. He changed my style of parenting, from letting my child control me, to me confidently guiding my child. He emphasized my roles as a wife and mother and prompted me to make them top priorities… second only to my faith. He granted me new work opportunities/hours that better suited my family. He blessed me with the capability to become biblically financially responsible (something I had always struggled with). Tithing and saving were now regular habits as I fully believed everything belonged to Him in the first place. Also to my great surprise, He placed special writing projects upon my heart, and led me to self-publish a series of children's books celebrating the local community and witnessing all at the same time. Not only had I become clay in

His hands, but now He was using me (little "worthless" me) to mold others! The fact that He trusted me in this manner was beyond humbling.

As the life-transforming events continued to unfold, my husband and I were united in marriage and then given the blessing of another beautiful child, this time a healthy baby boy. Needless to say, this second pregnancy experience went quite differently than the first. Both my husband and I were spilling over with gratitude as our little family of three became a family of four. Unity seemed to encompass our lives. Although we of course still experienced the normal struggles of raising children and dealt with issues stemming from our step-family/divorce situation, we faced it all together. We pressed on and trusted the Lord with every detail of our lives. We knew we had sought His will from the beginning, and that obedience allowed us to live without regret. He had brought us together, joined us in marriage, fulfilled our desire to bring a child into this world and we knew we were on His track because it had all started with prayer. At face value, my first marriage/child bearing experience might have appeared similar, but the difference was in the leader. The difference was in the commitment to seek the Lord's will BEFORE marrying and BEFORE bearing a child (before doing anything, really). I had specifically asked the Lord to choose my new husband for me and to guide me in all matters. Not only had I asked Him to choose my future husband, but I had asked him to lead me away from the tempting arms of all others who showed false interest in my life. I had fully realized that living life my own way had always caused everything to fall apart. As I now tried my hardest to live life God's way, there was nothing left to second guess. What a blessing it was to live securely in the arms of God's will. No more floundering aimlessly. No more sense of being lost.

By the time my daughter turned six and my new son turned one, yet another unimaginable and inconceivable turn of events took place. My father, who I had had very little to do with during my adult years, passed away at the age of sixty-two years. This event stirred a lot of emotions in my heart and brought my past relationship with him full circle. Needless to say, I had held onto a lot of resentment towards him over the years, yet even with all the turmoil surrounding our relationship he had chosen to show his love for me through a final small financial gift upon his death. He certainly didn't have to make me a beneficiary to his belongings and he could've changed that status at any moment, but he didn't. Though I had never felt this way before, I realized he evidently valued me and my family enough to offer us this life-changing gift in spite of our years of adult separation. Between him choosing to offer this gift, and through meeting so many of his adoring friends and extended family at his celebration of life, I had a new perspective of him. I now saw him as a friend to many and a confidant to even more. He had been a life-long encourager for the underdogs of this world and no one he had touched ever forgot his kindness. He had a huge, giving heart; something I had not witnessed in our strained father/daughter relationship. Though I'll never understand why it was easier for him to show physical love and emotion to people outside of his immediate family, it no longer mattered to me. I was at peace with him and now he too was finally at peace.

Additionally, my beautiful grandmother chose to offer a similar financial blessing upon her passing as well. Together, the combined financial gifts were just enough for my husband and I to financially restructure our lives and to allow me to fulfill the calling God was placing upon mine and my husband's heart. We now believed without a doubt, the best career I could undertake, was that of a stay-at-home wife and mother! Never in my wildest dreams did I imagine this would be possible, but once again, God had a definite plan for my life. He knew one of the most effective ways to strengthen my marriage and my family was for me to be available to my husband and children twenty-four hours a day, seven days a week. This inconceivable blessing completely changed the dynamic of our family, not to mention the total pace of our lives.

As my little boy was then taken out of daycare, we saw significant changes in his health and development. He was no longer subjected to constant colds and viruses, and went from being sick every few weeks, to only once in the year that followed. Also by becoming his sole educator, I was able to support and stimulate his learning processes in a much more effective manner. My daughter's life was also greatly affected. I was now minutes away if she became sick at school and she had my undivided attention and affection before and after school as well as all throughout summer break. Aside from the effects on my two children, my husband was also given a healthy dose of peace of mind. He no longer had to worry about whether his wife and children would get home safe in inclement weather or if his employer would be frustrated with him for taking an unexpected leave of absence when his family was ill. Every aspect of our day to day lives changed literally overnight once we redefined the rolls within our family. We actually felt as though we were diverting back to a much more old-fashioned way of living; my husband became the primary financial leader and I fulfilled my natural calling as a nurturer. As I had been raised in an era that screamed "woman can and should do it all" (i.e. get married, have children and work outside the home), this way of life had not previously been a goal of mine. Now after seeing how it transformed my family (and through learning the biblical importance of this type of a structure) it has become the way of life I'll most definitely try to impress upon my children as they grow up and make their own life choices. Of course their education will still be of utmost importance, but there are higher callings for which a paper degree cannot be obtained; one of which is "mother".

Still another area of my life God turned inside out was my ongoing battle with grief. I had spent more years grieving the loss of immediate family members, than I had actually physically spent with them. The loss of my mother when I was just ten years old, and the loss of my brother when I was seventeen years old had driven lasting daggers deep into my heart. I couldn't even begin to calculate how much time I'd spent in my life building fictional scenarios based on "what life might be like if they were still here". They had crossed my mind and caused an aching in my heart nearly every single day since their deaths and that timeframe now spanned decades. It had just always seemed I was only capable of focusing on my deep feeling of being "robbed" by their short lives and never on the ultimate gift they received; eternal life! As always, my selfish nature had made their deaths all about me and how that affected my life. Now, I was beginning to ask new questions…other than the same old "why". What about the outcome of their lives? What about the fact they were both devoted Christians and that there wasn't a doubt in the world as to where they had been taken. There's that word again, "taken". "Taken" began to take on a whole new meaning for me. As I studied the bible and truly realized all that lies ahead for believers, I formed a completely new outlook. In fact, while pondering these events for the millionth time, the Lord placed a final command on my heart: It was time…time to stop grieving. It was time to REJOICE and CELEBRATE! It was time to stop focusing on the pain created by their deaths, and to start focusing on the fact they had ever lived and had been precious parts of my life. The burden of grief in my life had now been eased. Though only two of my five original family members were still here on earth, I was at peace with all of them.

Eight: New Life

With all that had taken place after finally putting my faith first, I felt as though I had become two different people: One person before devoting my life to Christ and another after devoting my life to Christ. If someone would've told me five years earlier just how much my life was going to change, I would've fallen to my knees in laughter. Now, I was falling to my knees in thanksgiving. I was simply in awe of the many blessings in my life and I never dreamt I would make it this far down the road. Everything I had deemed impossible, and more, had become a reality. Because I had given my life to Christ, He had given me a new heart. He had taken my pain, grief, brokenness and shame and washed them away. Though I certainly hadn't forgotten my past, it no longer controlled me and I was free from it all. I was free to move forward. I had meaning, purpose, value and most importantly, I had HOPE.

I don't claim to have a perfect life (and I never will), but I do have a transformed life! I now choose everyday to let the Lord lead me as I do my best to follow His will. Of course I still make plenty of mistakes, but day by day and year by year I continue to improve and grow stronger as a wife, a mother, a friend and as a Christian. By putting my faith first and counting my blessings often I have thankfully been able to stay on track. To my shear delight, the old immoral ways of living are gone and the heartaches have been eased. Though I realize there will be many more trials in this life on earth, never again will I feel as though I'm facing them alone. Never again will I let heartache and shame consume me or break me. Never again will I let the ways of this world swallow me up and lead me astray. My eyes are now focused on eternity and I live every day in joyful anticipation, knowing what ultimately lies ahead. Finally, a true sense of peace has taken up residence in my soul, and that peace carries me onward reinforcing my renewed strength and HOPE. I give thanks to the Lord and stand in humble amazement. For He has taken over my life and brought me back to my baptismal roots, back to those early years of simple and joyful living that I thought were gone forever. I wake up. I play. I eat. I get scrubbed clean. I sleep. Repeat. LIFE IS SIMPLE. LIFE IS FULL OF HOPE!

$\mathcal{N}ine$: The Final Act

As I've now publically exposed my journey with and without Christ in my life, I wish to make my motives known and clear. I do not offer any of this information to gain pity or praise, and I am not here to boast about anything I have done, right or wrong. My choices to bare my deepest pain and shame, are based on my ultimate desire to help the countless men and women who still walk that familiar road of sinful, broken, or grief-stricken living. My openness is for the troubled souls of this world who have carried their weight too far and too long. I ask you this: When will you choose to finally break the cycle and experience what God's best is for you? I pray that time is now as a transformed life awaits all those who will finally choose to change their ways and trust in the Lord. If you can relate in any way to my journey, rest assured the message of this book is for you. Many prayers have surrounded the birth of this book and the purpose is clear: Broken lives do not have to remain broken!

It is my sincere prayer that God would use my own broken and now healed life to give others HOPE; HOPE for their own life-transformation! Through sincere repentance and commitment to faith, God can mend what hurts and transform what lacks if only He is invited to do so. Are you ready to finally put the past behind you and begin a new journey? Are you ready to have the weight lifted from your shoulders and carried by the Lord? Are you willing to invite the Lord into the driver's seat of your life and finally move beyond all the hurtful words and situations you acknowledged during the self-examination process? If you are, I promise you will not only be given a new set of words and situations to define your existence, but you will also be given a new heart and a new life in Christ. For the Lord loves to take what is broken and make it beautiful!

If you are truly ready to take this leap of faith, I ask that you would start your journey by praying the prayer that changed my own life:

Heavenly Father, you know the pain and weight I carry in my life and I now realize I cannot move forward and break this cycle without you. I have lived my life by my own worldly standards and I've watched it all fall apart time and time again. My sin, shame and despair have held me hostage for far too long and I need YOU! I need you to pick up the broken pieces of my life and show me a new way. I am so very sorry for all the ways I have hurt and disobeyed you and I desire more than anything to live for you and to put my trust in you. Please direct my steps and open my heart to receive you, so that I may finally experience your best for me, which ultimately includes the precious gift of eternal life won on the cross through the death and resurrection of your son, Jesus Christ. In His Holy name I pray, Amen.

As you go forth from this moment in time, I pray you will begin to experience a new set of emotions, feelings, and concepts to define your existence. Though you know there will always be trials and tribulations in this life, your sincere invitation to walk with the Lord will never leave you walking alone again. Day by day and year by year, God's best will begin to fall into place in your new life. Though it may take time and patience to be able to circle and accept into your life all of the positive new words below, I pray there is at least one word you are able to circle today:

~HOPE~

Forgiveness	Honesty	Trust
Peace	Value	Purpose
Integrity	Comfort	Selflessness
Modesty	Strength	Sincerity
Confidence	Triumph	Boldness
Faithfulness	Gratitude	Commitment
Perseverance	Humility	Honor
Patience	Grace	Prosperity
Conviction	Love	Unity

May God bless you in your journey!